LET'S PRETEND

By the author of

GAMES BABIES PLAY

MORE GAMES BABIES PLAY

TRAVELING GAMES FOR BABIES

LET'S PRETEND

Games of Fantasy for Babies and Young Children

Julie Hagstrom

Illustrations by Christiane Stalland

A & W Visual Library • New York

A & W Publishers, Inc.
95 Madison Avenue
New York, N.Y. 10016

Library of Congress Catalog Card Number: 81-66196

ISBN: 0–89104–269–5

Designed by Jane Preston

Printed in the United States of America

This book is for Amy,
who opened up our world
and our minds with her imagination
and love of adventure.

CONTENTS

✣✣✣✣✣

INTRODUCTION

Here is a book filled with games and ideas for encouraging pretend play in your very young children. And, just as *Games Babies Play* and *More Games Babies Play* share the games we played with our daughters Amy and Katie, *Let's Pretend* recalls Amy's earliest imaginary play, the games that later became her favorites and the games that best suited little sister Katie, struggling to keep up but unable to even talk.

It's hard to say when a parent can incorporate make-believe or fantasy into a child's play time. The most likely time would be somewhere between the second and third birthday, because of the increasing language proficiency during this stage. But those babies and toddlers fortunate enough to have older children around will have an early introduction not only to sandbox pies, kitchen play, and crayons, but also to the mystifying behavior of pretend play. Babies, being more observant than we give them credit for, soon catch on to sipping tea from empty cups and shaking their fingers "No, no!" to stuffed bears. We remember when Katie, around 12- or 15-months-old, began to smack her lips and wag her head in a highly imitative fashion while holding Amy's fake grapes from the grocery cart close to her mouth. Watch your toddler for signs of pretend play and then encourage her with some of the games designed for children under three.*

Most children enjoy pretending, flowing into it easily with an "I know what! Let's pretend this is my house and you call me up!" or "Pretend I'm Tigger and I bounce into your garden!" We grownups have a more difficult time of it—being embarrassed in the supermarket as other shoppers watch us shrink back in terror from the lion in the frozen foods. Being scolded in the park by my daughter, pretending to be my mommy, I avoid eye contact with the other park visitors and sulk over to the bench, punished for throwing sand. Even waiting in line at Disneyland, I self-consciously whisper my lines in Amy's game of Peter Pan. Annoyed at my lack of enthusiasm she cries, "Mommy! Say it louder!" How wonderful to be so spontaneous and open! And it's worth encouraging this kind of play, even at the cost of receiving suspicious glances from passers-by, because as children get older, and especially after they start school, their play will become more structured and more conscious of the values and opinions of their friends.

*Since our daughters are the inspiration for this book, I've used "she" and "her" throughout.

It's my hope that by giving my children a variety of experiences in pretending, both realistic and absurd, they'll be able to play games as well as approach problems creatively when they're older. Perhaps showing them that a chair can be a boat, house, or open-mouthed crocodile; or that a towel can be a cape or magic carpet, will teach them to keep their minds open and look for all the options available to them when making decisions later in life. We'll have to wait and see, but one thing I know for sure is that at the ages of four, and one-and-a-half, fantasy play is a great deal of fun!

Realistic fantasy play—playing doctor, fireman or restaurant—has an advantage in that it provides an awareness of ordinary events or situations. In order to play, a child has to recall what she's seen or been told. And if she gets bogged down in the game you can pass along some bits of information to make the game more enjoyable. When Amy, age two-and-a half, played "kitty" she would get a bowl of water and a bowl of food (Cheerios) and scratch the door to go out. Not having any cats, this was the extent of Amy's knowledge about them, and the game soon became boring. So, I introduced the scratching post, kitty door and, what else, the litter box! Amy loved it and began to watch for cats to see what else she could add to her game.

But if you really want to know what your child has on her mind, put her in a role-play situation, letting her be the mommy or daddy—and don't act so surprised! Where do you think she heard that! Listening to kids play "school" will tell you all you need to know without a teacher conference, and if you really want to know what went on with the babysitter last Saturday, just play a game about it!

The following are games that Amy and Katie played when they were in the mood to pretend. Sometimes Amy felt like planning ahead for a make-believe circus, sometimes she wanted to play "house" or "market," and other times she'd get a spontaneous idea and be off in a world where anything can happen. So try a little of each with your child, always helping a realistic player accept the impossible and showing an overly imaginative player the fun in true-to-life play! Come, then, let's pretend!

LET'S PRETEND

PART 1

In the Beginning

Since it's debatable how much your baby under three will understand, begin slowly and simply. When Katie first started to walk, pushing a buggie, stroller or shopping cart, we would say, "Oh! Bye-bye! Are you Mommy? Going to the market?" Apparently she understood enough of those simple words to pick up on the game and she would seriously wave "bye-bye," then toddle out of the room. Hitching a purse up over her shoulder and marching toward the front door is another favorite trick of most toddlers. It's a first attempt at role-playing, so encourage her with words she knows. Asking, "Do you have your *keys*?" or calling, "Don't forget your *hat*!" really caught Katie's attention, making the game more fun for all. The games you'll find in this section span almost a two-year period. If you're playing with an 18-month-old, much of the conversation will be one-sided, but don't worry, she's listening!

When your little one first becomes involved in pretend play she'll seem to take it very seriously. We still laugh, thinking of Katie trying to look grown-up and sophisticated during a mock birthday party. Her Big Bird birthday hat was in place, the playdough cake was on the table and she sipped pretend punch. The look on her face was stone serious until I caught her eye, and then the bright twinkle told me, "I know it's just for fun, Mom!" What a funny baby.

Babies imitate the people around them, so play alongside your toddler, letting her follow your example step-by-step. And show her it's fun—laugh and hug often! For young players, two- to three-years-old, monsters, witches, or even crocodiles can sometimes be too scary, pretend or not. If yours is a daring player, go ahead and give her a little excitement, but don't overdo it!

These first games are designed to help your child feel comfortable pretending, and to help her discover that her own ideas can make the games even more fun. Set an example by adding your own personal touch to the games; and when your young player contributes an idea, accept it gladly into the game. It may be difficult to add "and the couch is a huge ship" to a game of dress up, but remember it *is* pretend and anything goes!

Here are the games that Amy and Katie played in the beginning. . . .

❧ 1 ❧
Dress Up

Equipment: Any assortment of old purses, hats, necklaces, and bracelets. A mirror (full-length is best).

Position: Sit or kneel in front of the box, drawer or cupboard where equipment is stored.

Procedure:
1. Introduce one item at a time, demonstrating how to use it yourself. Say, "Look at the pretty necklace! Mommy's going to wear this one."
2. Then encourage your partner to follow your example. "Here, does Katie want to wear a necklace?" Loop it over her head, exclaiming how pretty she looks.
3. If she's enjoying herself, go on to purses or hats. Repeat steps one and two.
4. If she seems unsure of the game, or doesn't want to get dressed up herself, that's okay. Go ahead and show her what the whole ensemble looks like on you (hat, purse, bracelet, etc.)
5. Admire yourself in the mirror.
6. Select a new hat or purse for yourself, showing her how the activity continues.
7. Encourage your little player to also find something new, helping her pick it out if necessary.
8. Continue dressing up, looking in the mirror and laughing at your silly selves until her interest span is exhausted.

Suggestions: If you're going to add waving "bye-bye," or rushing off to pretend parties, just be sure your child is old enough to understand it's not for real! There's nothing sadder than the poor toddler who bursts into tears when mommy, in her enthusiasm for the game, waves and calls "bye-bye!"

Some fun items to add later, when you both become experts, are old scarves, aprons, or dresses.

Variations: Using only big shoes, mommy's or daddy's, can be fun in itself. But be careful of high heels and twisted ankles!

🌿 2 🌿
Tea Party

Equipment: Toy tea cups, plates, and pitcher (silverware optional).

Position: Set the equipment on a child's table (a quilt spread out on the floor works just as well for picnickers). Seat yourself at the table with your child next to you.

Procedure:
1. Begin by serving your child some water in her cup. Say, "Hello! Would you like some tea?"
2. Pour some for yourself, "Oh, yes. I'm having some too!"
3. Sipping the "tea" daintily, encourage your player to follow suit (if she hasn't already).
4. At this point feel free to ad-lib, saying that the tea is too hot (blow on it gently), needs sugar or even tastes terrible (blah!).
5. Let your child serve second helpings, with or without your aid, depending on her age.
6. Moving along to the main course, pretend to sample cake, pudding, yogurt, or any favorite fun food from the plate in front of you. Say, "Oh! I love this cherry pie! Have you tasted it? Ummmm good!"
7. Your child may choose to just watch you (not about to make a fool of *herself*) but try to get her to join in.
8. Every so often, especially if your young player looks confused, lean over and whisper, "How funny! It's just pretend! It's a game. Is this a fun game?" and laugh at yourselves.
9. Again, ad-libbing as you go, pretend the food is cold or hot, good or bad.
10. When your little player loses interest just say, "Party all done!"

Suggestions: If your child is confused by the mention of food when no food is present, you can always use snack cereal or crackers until she understands the principle of pretending.

Variations: When your child has passed the everything-in-the-mouth stage you can play with small pretend foods. Tiny oranges, bananas, and bunches of grapes can be bought at most toy stores.

At the beach or in the sandbox, sandpies with leaves or sticks as decorations are great for tea parties.

And, of course, once playdough can be safely introduced (around age two) any number of delicacies can be baked for a party.

❧ 3 ❧
Mama's Baby (*Daddy's Baby)

Equipment: Baby buggy or stroller, a doll, a doll's blanket, and a bottle.

Position: Inside or out, place doll in buggy.

Procedure:
1. Draw your child's attention to the buggy and baby by saying, "Look! Your baby wants to go for a walk. Push your baby!"
2. After she has pushed the stroller a short way say, "Uh oh! Is your baby crying? You'd better pick her up for a minute." Demonstrate by picking up the doll yourself if she doesn't respond.
3. A few "Ohhhs and Ahhhs" or "It's okays" fit in nicely when comforting the doll.
4. As the soothed doll is put back into its buggy, remind your child to cover her "baby" up with the blanket.
5. After she's pushed the buggy a bit further, once again pretend you hear the doll cry.
6. This time suggest your little player try giving her "baby" a bottle.
7. Continue along, stopping occasionally to comfort the fussy doll, until your child tires of the game.

Suggestions: Be sure you have enough room for your child to easily maneuver her buggy around in. If she's constantly bumping into furniture or catching the wheels on corners, the game will become too frustrating. It's best played outside, along the sidewalk from one corner to the other.

Regardless of the wide variety of dolls available, we found that the favorites were the nice, fat, middle-sized dolls made out of soft rubber, hair or no hair. Only one outfit is necessary because it will probably be stripped of its clothes most of the time anyway!

Variations: *If you're playing Daddy's Baby with a little boy and no dolls are handy, a teddy bear pulled in a wagon works just as well.

When Katie got the hang of the game she had her own ideas to add. She used to shake her finger and shout "No, no! Baby!" in her bossiest voice, then chuckle to herself. So anytime your little player strikes out on her own, play along!

✂ 4 ✂
Here a Horse, There a Horse

Equipment: In this purely imaginative game your child's "horse" can be anything from the arm of a chair to a pillow, your leg, a log, or a low tree branch!

Position: Help your child straddle her "horse" as you hold her around the waist.

Procedure:
1. First you need to find a horsie. Say, "Do you want to go for a horsie ride? Hop on my foot and let's go!"
2. Let your child bounce on your foot (legs crossed) a few minutes, then come to a stop with a "Whoa, horsie!"
3. Looking around the room, yard, or campground, encourage your little player to find another horsie, "This horse is too slow! Let's find another horse."
4. Give her a chance to find a "horse" before suggesting the arm of the couch or side of the tub. If she comes up with a rideable idea—great! If not, steer her in your direction saying, "Hey, maybe you could ride this! He looks pretty fast. Think you can handle him?"
5. Once mounted, go through the usual giddy-up-go routine, pretending to be riding around the room ("Look out for the TV, horsie!")
6. After a little while suggest that this poor horse is tired, and look for a fresh mount!
7. Remember to ham it up, making the little rider forget she's not on the real thing!
8. Continue your horse-hopping, accepting your child's suggestions enthusiastically.

Suggestions: To make the game livelier, ask your child to name the horse and then help her describe the horse. Ask, "Where's the tail? Where are his eyes?" And of course each horse should have its own personality, from tired old hag to spirited young colt!

   This game helps pass the time when waiting for grandma to arrive.

Variations: Instead of finding horses in the strangest places, you and your child can look for likely boats (the bed is a natural) or cars (a dining-room chair, for starters).

✹ 5 ✹
Monster—Katie's Favorite

Equipment: None

Position: Sit or stand facing your child.

Procedure:
1. Call to your child, "Do you know what a monster says?" Then follow with a loud, but not scary "Ahhhhh!" Stretch out your arms and wiggle your fingers for effect.
2. Laugh and ask, "Can *you* be a monster? Let's hear Katie be a monster!"
3. As she imitates your monster sounds, gasp in fear, pull back and say, "Oh! You scared me!"
4. Most likely, this reaction will delight your little player and send her into uncontrollable giggles. Katie enjoyed the reaction so much that her monster sounds became her opening remark to family visitors and passers-by alike!
5. Ask her to repeat her monster act. And again cringe back in terror.
6. Instruct her to go show another member of the family her scary monster. Be sure the person about to be attacked has overheard or already knows the game, so the correct reaction will be given.

Variations: Stage a monster attack right back at your little monster and see her jump!
A follow-up tickle can catch a monster off guard and result in a lot of laughter.

✖ 6 ✖
Here Kitty, Kitty, Kitty!

Equipment: Two small unbreakable bowls, Cherrios (optional).

Procedure:
1. Suggest to your little player that she play "kitty." Say, "Can you walk on your hands and knees like a kitty cat?"
2. Once she is in position, find out just how much she knows about cats. Ask, "What do kitties say? Can you meow like a kitty.?"
3. Give her the lead in the game by asking, "What else do cats do?" If you have a family cat your child will already know the basics. Start out with what cats eat and drink. At this point your player can use the two bowls, Cherrios and water, to simulate cat food and milk.
4. Explain how a cat laps milk and let her try it!
5. Talk about how cats tend to scratch on furniture to sharpen their claws. Amy spent a lot of time being the naughty cat scratching on the good sofa while my part was to say crossly, "No, no! Kitty!"
6. Then pretend you've been to the pet store and bought a scratching post! This could be anything from a book tossed on the floor to an imaginary area in the room.
7. As long as she is interested, continue introducing new facets of a cat's life. There's the cat door (you could drape a towel over a chair or coffee table), the litter box (the details are up to you!), collars and, of course, grooming.
8. Once basic pet care is taken care of, you can explain some of the more personal likes and dislikes of cats. Calling, "Here kitty, kitty, kitty," scratch her between the ears (a good trick) and let her rub up against your legs. Whether or not you want to mention curling up on laps is up to you!
9. Depending on the age and sensitivity of your child, you may want to mention how cats chase mice and birds. But it's a bit sticky when asked, "What do they do when they catch them?"
10. And you can always end up with a good ol' cat nap!

Suggestions: It would take several different sessions to complete all ten steps of Here Kitty, Kitty, Kitty, so just use what interests your child and add anything that comes to mind.

Use this game when you're busy cooking, cleaning, or gardening, because it will keep your little one happy while you get something accomplished.

Variations: It doesn't have to be a cat, you know. You can do the same thing with dogs (don't forget the dog house) or fish in a fish bowl!

13

PART 2

When I Grow Up

Have you ever noticed that while the grownups are reminiscing about childhood days their children are often in the other room pretending to be grownups? No matter how many times you tell them it's hard or boring, being a grownup is the fantasy of all young children. And role-playing various occupations is a natural way to encourage pretend play.

The occupations your youngster is interested in will depend on her personal experiences and your influence. What follows are a few all-time favorites, as well as the one Amy and Katie especially enjoy. However, you'll discover many more as you and your child become aware of people and their jobs. Amy became fascinated with storerooms and spent her first moments in any store hunting for "the backroom where only the workers can go." She inevitably came out of stores with interesting bits of information that, as she would explain, "a worker told me."

The conventional jobs like doctor, teacher, or fireman can get your child started, but don't forget other jobs such as telephone operator, librarian, or carpet cleaner.

The use of props is optional. Some occupations are more fun if you have the proper equipment (medical kit for playing doctor or comb and curlers for beauty shop) but, since it is pretend, most kids will be satisfied with imaginary hoses and ropes for fireman and cowboy!

You will be a leading player when a game is first played. Even if your child has friends to play with, she and her friends will need someone to guide them through the first few times. Later she will instigate the game herself, either playing alone or with siblings and friends.

Doctor, Doctor, Hurry Quick!

Equipment: Toy doctor kit.

Position: Patient lies on a couch while doctor and/or nurse (depending on number of players) stand next to the "examining table." The first time around it works best if you are the doctor, so that when you trade places your child will have an example to follow.

Procedure:
1. Doctor must first ask patient (who can be moaning softly) what's wrong.
2. Response will probably depend on the latest visit to the doctor ("the flu," "just a check up" or "ear infection" are common answers).
3. Doctor then proceeds to examine patient with various toy instruments. Check the heart rate and blood pressure with the appropriate "Ah hahs!" and "Hmmmms."
4. Be sure to check the throat ("Say Ahhh!"), eyes ("How many fingers do you see?"), and reflexes.
5. With a worried face, the doctor makes a diagnosis, which invariably includes a shot!
6. In administering the shot say, "This is going to hurt for just a second!" as opposed to "This won't hurt at all." It would be a shame to have the game backfire on you some day.
7. At this point patient and doctor can trade places and start all over again.

Suggestions: Remind your children that girls can be doctors, just as boys can be nurses.

Variations: Broken bones and casts are fascinating to children, at least to those fortunate enough not to have had the real thing! Toilet paper wrapped around a limb could be the cast, and a hobbyhorse (the kind on a stick) works as a makeshift crutch. The game can be played at the "hospital," starting with the ambulance ride itself.

Many of the doctor's instruments can be adapted to dentistry or even a veterinarian's practice.

❧ 8 ❧
Letter Carrier

Equipment: Envelopes, stamps (stickers, Christmas Seals, etc,—all optional).

Procedure:
1. Decide who is letter carrier and who is receiving letters.
2. Determine what will be the mailbox, or delivery drop-off point. If you are playing outside it might be a tree trunk or fence railing. Inside areas could include a chair, table, or shelf.
3. Letter carrier "drives" or walks to mailbox area and leaves a letter. She then continues on her rounds delivering imaginary mail.
4. Other player comes "to check her mailbox" and finds the letter.
5. Receiver of the letter exclaims "Oh, a letter from my grandma!" or "Oh, no! Just another bill!"
6. Receiver then puts a new letter into mailbox that she wants letter carrier to pick up.
7. Letter carrier returns to mailbox and picks up the letter to go to the post office. Letter carrier can also deliver another letter to receiver if she wants.
8. Letter carrier returns to main post office (kitchen? tree stump?) and picks up more letters to take out on her "route."
9. At this point you can change places and repeat steps one through eight, or continue on with steps ten through fifteen. If this is your first time playing Letter Carrier, changing roles now, before you add more steps, will help everyone become more familiar with the game.
10. On her next round the letter carrier could deliver an imaginary package (or a box of some sort). In this case she must go to the door and knock.
11. When receiver answers, letter carrier must have her sign for the package.
12. After letter carrier leaves, receiver decides to write a letter, stamps it, and places it in her mailbox for the letter carrier to pick up.
13. This time around letter carrier ignores receiver's house!
14. Receiver must run "outside" and call to letter carrier, "Hey! I have a letter here for you to pick up!"

Procedure: **15.** Letter carrier then explains that the flag on her mailbox wasn't raised.
16. Now trade roles and go back to step one. Pick new mailboxes, too!

Suggestions: If your child gets stuck in her role as either letter carrier or receiver, just whisper her part to her, let her repeat it, and continue on.

Using real postal terms such as route, zip code, delivery, UPS, or mail service makes the game fun.

Variations: There are as many variations for this game as there are children who play it. Each player will add her own touch, slightly changing the format—that's what pretending is all about! You can try delivering mail in rain or snow, or the receiver could have a huge dog that chases the letter carrier!

❧ 9 ❧

Fire Fighter to the Rescue

Equipment: None. (Hat and hose are optional)

Procedure: 1. Let your player decide whether she wants to be the fire fighter or the person *needing* the fire fighter.
2. Again, let your young player figure out where the fire station as well as the house with the fire will be located.
3. Player who is not fire fighter pretends to be cooking, reading, or sleeping. . . .
4. Suddenly, she discovers the house is on fire. This can be done by hearing a smoke alarm, smelling, or seeing the fire.
5. Player rushes to the phone, pretends to call the fire department (ask operator to connect you, then give your address) and then grabs her children (dolls) and rushes out. When we played, it just so happened that the house always caught on fire when daddy was at work or out running!
6. Meanwhile, the fire department receives the emergency phone call and jumps into the fire engine, siren blaring (allow a lot of "Wow, wow, wow" sound effects here).
7. Fire fighter pretends to drive her engine through town (down the hall and through the dining room?) running red lights and all.
8. Once at the burning house, she pretends to unwind her hose, hook it up to the hydrant and squirt the house while the other player watches and says things like, "Oh, dear, I can't imagine how it started! Hurry, put out the fire!"
9. Fire fighter can finish putting out the fire and go back to the station, at which point the two players can change roles and start over.
10. If you and your child are experienced players, add to the game by pretending to rescue someone from a second-story window (a kitchen step stool is a handy prop for this part of the game).
11. Player with burning house can double as person to be rescued. Remember to ham it up and let the fire fighter try to "carry" you down her ladder.

Procedure: 12. Continue with any new ideas your child has or wind up the game with the hero fire fighter being interviewed by the local newspaper.

Suggestions: After your first time playing Fire Fighter to the Rescue discuss all the different ways a fire can start. This is a good way to teach your little one fire prevention rules.

Next time you see a fire truck check it over carefully. Look over your neighborhood for fire hydrants.

Variations: If you have a Lego or Fisher Price fire house set up, the game can be played using them.

If you have more than two players it's easy to add more crew members to the fire department or more burning buildings.

❧ 10 ❧
Mr. and Mrs. Fix-It

Equipment: None. (Screw driver, pliers and tape are optional).

Procedure:
1. Ask your young player to think of a household item that could break down.
2. Then, let her choose whether she wants to be the repair person or the one in need of help.
3. Repair person finds a spot for her "shop."
4. Person at home discovers a broken appliance, furniture, or whatever. "Here I am putting the dirty clothes in the washer. . . . Oh, no! The water is squirting all over!"
5. She rushes to the phone to call a repair person (pretend to check in the Yellow Pages first). "Ring, ring!"
6. Repair person answers, "Mr. and Mrs. Fix-It, Mrs. Fix-It speaking."
7. Person with the broken washer explains the problem and Mrs. Fix-It says she'll be right over.
8. "Ding, dong!" Mrs. Fix-It arrives at a pretend door and is shown to the broken washer.
9. After many "Uh ohs" and "Oh dears" Mrs. Fix-It announces it's the fan belt, motor, or spark plug!
10. At this point Mrs. Fix-It repairs the washer, working with either real or imaginary tools. Tape is a good "tool" because it comes off easily and is fun to play with. Amy enjoys tape because her daddy often resorts to it as a home remedy!
11. Once the appliance is repaired Mrs. Fix-It presents her bill, giving a few last-minute instructions, "Don't turn the handle so hard" or, "Be sure to put oil on this part!"
12. Other player pays her bill muttering, "Gee, one hundred dollars just to fix a simple leak!"

Suggestions: This game is most successful if you've recently had a repair person to your home.

Variations: After having our carpets cleaned we played Carpet Cleaner. This game can be adapted to any kind of worker who comes to your home, window washer (this actually gets something accomplished), construction worker, or painter.

   Before calling Mr. and Mrs. Fix-It, try to repair the broken item yourself, only making it worse!

   Let *Mr.* Fix-It answer the phone and take the job.

❧ 11 ❧
Hairdos

Equipment: Hairbrush, comb, squirt bottle filled with water, towel, and hand mirror.

Position: Sit on the floor while your child stands behind you, or sit in a chair while your child stands on a stool or chair behind you.

Procedure:
1. Tuck towel around your neck—just like the real thing!
2. Pretending you have come to get your hair cut, begin by saying, "Oh, I'm glad I could get an appointment today! My hair is driving me crazy!"
3. Barber/beautician asks, "How do you want it done?" If this is your first time playing, just whisper the barber's lines to her!
4. Getting into the spirit of the game, explain that you want it short on the sides or curly on the top!
5. Barber/beautician begins by squirting hair lightly with water bottle, then combs it through.
6. From here on let your little hair stylist twist and turn your hair to her liking.
7. Let her trim your hair, too, using pretend "hand scissors" and "click, click" sound effects.
8. Holding up the hand mirror, react to your new hairdo. "Oh I love it!" or "Oh no! It's way too short. I look like a pin-head!" or, "Could you curl this side a little and trim some off the back?"
9. At this point you can trade places, but most young players prefer to give the hairdo rather than get one. If she's still interested, start over as if you're a new customer.

Suggestions: This game gives you a chance to watch TV or get caught up on the newspaper. It isn't one you'll want to play if you've just had your hair done.

Variations: For players with longer hair, you can add curlers and/or clips to the equipment list.
 Play Hairdos in the bath, making fancy styles out of shampoo suds! If no one is in the mood to play Hairdos, your eager beautician can practice on a doll.

PART 3

❧❀❦

Show Time

Last year Amy knew "Jingle Bells" by heart and was constantly putting on her black Mary Janes so she could dance and sing this song that would be the grand finale at the preschool Christmas show. Her home demonstrations were precious, the small husky voice off key just enough to be cute, blue eyes sparkling and hands clapping. But the home movies of the actual performance told a different story. She never opened her mouth once, never sang one word, hummed a hum, or clapped a clap. We have ten minutes of Amy, motionless in a crowd of faces, biting her nails!

Stage fright is a terrible disappointment and it happens to the best of us. But at home, among family and friends, performing even the most difficult of routines is always fun! I think we all have had fantasies of being the star of stage and screen—the house lights dim and the spotlight is on us! And children, being natural hams, have a real ball with this kind of pretend play.

Again, the kinds of performances your child will want to imitate depend on her experiences. My husband, a junior high school teacher, is often asked to attend dance rehearsals, orchestra recitals, or gymnastic meets in which his students are performing. He usually takes Amy along and sure enough, the next day Amy will emerge in tights and dress shoes, or with tambourine and recorder, and announce, "We're having a show!"

Props or costumes are minimal—whatever's handy around the house. Announcing the acts is an integral part of the shows and it was Amy's idea to use a carrot for a microphone!

In Show Time play, other than helping your child set up or dress up, your main role is as audience—to laugh or gasp in response to the action and to encourage the little performer with an "Encore" and "Bravo!"

✹12✹

Circus Acts

Equipment: None

Procedure: 1. Explain that a circus is a show with several different acts going on at the same time. Describe and demonstrate any three of your favorite circus acts and let your child perform them.
2. We always started with the popular lion tamer's act. You are the tamer first, with a pretend whip.
3. Your young partner can be the lion, or it can be imaginary.
4. Demonstrate the lion tamer's act, "Roar lion! Stand up lion! Jump through the ring of fire!"
5. Remember to crack your whip!
6. Then slip out of the cage just in the nick of time.
7. Now let your partner be the tamer.
8. Next, try the tightrope walker's act. Masking tape on the floor makes a good highwire, but it's optional.
9. Balancing yourself, teeter from one side to another as you pretend to walk the tightrope high in the big top!
10. Ride an imaginary bike on the wire.
11. You can even stage a heart-stopping fall.
12. Now it's your child's turn to try her luck on the highwire!
13. Clowns were always our favorite way to wind up Circus Acts. Begin by pantomiming a sad face suddenly changed to a happy face by a kiss from your child.
14. Your clown act can include any kind of silly stunt. Slipping on a banana peel, blowing up a balloon that pops, or just making silly faces make the clown's act a big hit.

Procedure: **15.** Now it's your child's turn to make you laugh!

16. If everyone is still in the mood, add other acts that you or your child are familiar with.

Suggestions: If you've seen a circus recently, use your child's favorite experiences and ideas as you play.

Variations: Now that Circus Acts has been introduced to your young performer, your main role will be as audience as she single-handedly puts on the acts!

Although Amy had never been to a circus, she did have a cousin who rode in horse shows. This experience was often combined with her circus acts.

❧ 13 ❧
Dance Recital*

Equipment: Record player, records, fancy dress shoes (optional).

Position: Seat yourself on the "audience" side of the room. Audience participation means you are the announcer as well as in charge of the record player!

Procedure:
1. Have your child select a record.
2. As announcer, introduce her "first number." "Ladies and Gentlemen! We are having a show! The first dance is Rubber Duckie."
3. As your little performer dances, be sure to "Ohhh" and "Ahhh" at any tricky steps or swirls. Clap spontaneously.
4. If your child hasn't had much exposure to dance performances, take a turn yourself and show her a few steps she can copy.
5. As long as she is happy performing, encourage her with claps, whistles and exclamations. Little side comments, "Oh, my! That looks hard!" really please small performers.
6. At the end of each number shout "Encore!" and "Bravo!"

Suggestions: Taking a child to a local dance school rehearsal will give her a much better idea of what it's all about.

Variations: If there are any siblings who want to join in let them take a turn. Eighteen-month-old Katie enjoyed stealing the show when Amy played Dance Recital.

Incorporating scarves into a dance makes a performer feel very grown-up.

*If dancing doesn't interest your player, encourage a gymnastics or—for the more macho types—a weight-lifting show. These, too, can be done to music.

❧ 14 ❧
Join the Parade

Equipment: Any assortment of musical instruments. Harmonicas, tambourines, and bells are the least expensive as well as the least nerve-wracking!

Procedure:
1. Each player selects an instrument.
2. To begin, you be the leader. Announce, "Let's have a parade! March with me!"
3. March around the room or yard chanting "We're in a parade. . . ."
4. Come to a halt and call out, "Just the tambourines!" As if performing for a sidewalk crowd, the tambourine player does a quick solo.
5. Give each player a chance to individually perform.
6. Making another circle around the room or yard, calling out, "Let's sing!" Pick a song you know she's familiar with, even if it's "Happy Birthday" or "Jingle Bells" in June!
7. Now let someone else lead and give the directions.

Suggestions: Pots, pans and spoons can easily be substituted for real instruments.
If your child enjoys making music you may want to get her Creative Playthings' Rhythm Band Set. But, be forewarned, it does have cymbals!
After your initial performance you will probably be transferred to the "audience." Kids pick this game up quickly and love adding their own ideas—remember, the more the merrier!

Variations: Put on a band record while marching.

❧ 15 ❧
Puppet Show

Equipment: Hand puppets of any size, shape, or color; a table, couch, or bed to serve as a partition for the players to crouch behind.

Procedure:

1. To introduce the game, let your child be the audience while you stage the show.
2. Get comfortable behind the partition, a puppet on each hand.
3. Have your "audience" find a good seat in the theatre.
4. Begin the show with an announcer: "Introducing the cute and cuddly Dancing Bears! Here's Bonnie Bear!"
5. Make Bonnie Bear reluctant to appear. Your other puppet can give her a push onto the stage.
6. Introduce your other hand.
7. This puppet bounds on stage full of confidence.
8. The puppets tell the audience a little about themselves but, of course, Bonnie Bear is too shy and her friend has to coax it out of her.
9. Remember to keep the puppets' heads, arms, and bodies moving with the conversation. Be sure they often look away from each other and out into the audience.
10. Making up a tune as you go, dance the puppets across the stage.
11. Bonnie Bear, however, trips and is too embarrassed to continue. Make her voice a touch whiney by now.
12. Your other puppet becomes disgusted with her, bops her on the head, and steals the show with some pretty incredible dance steps.
13. Puppets bow and slip off stage.
14. Let your audience have a turn at show biz now!
15. Help her get situated, puppets facing the right way, etc.
16. She will probably start out very much like you did—it's hard to know what to do!
17. When she gets stuck, ask the puppets questions from the audience. (What are your names, what song do you know. . . .")
18. No matter what the puppets do or say, applaud loudly and laugh heartily.

Suggestions: It's easier to make up a dialogue if the puppets have distinct personalities. Opposites are always good for a laugh—happy and sad, mean and nice, loud and quiet.

The puppets' "show" can consist of dancing, singing, joke telling, story telling, or just plain talking.

Variations: Four hands are better than two! If your child has friends over or Daddy's home, let two people work four puppets! It's hard to keep who's who straight, but it's a lot of fun, especially for older players.

If your group is TV oriented, they may want to change puppets and interrupt the show for a commercial message!

✸ 16 ✸

The Flying Linguini

An Acrobat Show with Daddy

Equipment: None

Procedure:
1. When your little one is in the mood to wrestle and rough house, first look for Daddy!
2. Let Daddy and his little tumbler warm up with a few minutes of unstructured wrestling and rolling around on the floor.
3. Now, introduce the idea of learning tricks for an acrobat show.
4. Try this one: Daddy lies on his back on the floor and lifts straightened legs to the height of your child's chest. Raise arms above head. Child leans chest against feet and reaches for Daddy's hands as Daddy lifts child up off the floor with his feet. Final position is child "floating" above Daddy, supported by his feet and arms. Lower slowly!
5. And this one: Again Daddy lies on his back, legs flat, and arms stretched out on the floor above his head. Child stands on Daddy's hands facing his legs. Daddy lifts child up as he brings his feet toward her to hold onto. Final position is almost a human wheel—child as the upper half and Daddy as lower half.
6. Once Daddy feels his troupe has mastered the routine, call the family together for a demonstration.
7. We used to hum what we referred to as "circus music" to add suspense to the show.
8. Many calls of Bravo wind up the act nicely.

Suggestions: Your child can easily get wound up playing Flying Linguini. We used to play just before bath, hoping the warm water would relax her before bed.

Be careful of the giggles! These stunts can be pretty funny—especially during practice.

Variations: Any fun acrobatic position you make up as you go along can be a regular part of the "act."

PART 4

✹✹✹✹

Back to Basics

Playing "house," "school," and "party" are favorites of all ages. In fact, the school-age child enjoys these games more than the preschooler. Of course, this older child has had more experience in these areas and delights in having the shoe on the other foot—even if it is just pretend!

Amy's earliest versions of "house" were very simplified. The chair would be her house, the couch mine, and she'd call me on a pretend phone to ask if I'd come visit. But when several neighborhood children gathered together the game took on a more complex dimension. An older player (five- or six-years-old) would usually set up the structure of the game, assigning roles and duties. In these situations you are merely an observer and occasional mediator. If you busy yourself watering the plants or changing bed sheets they won't think you're paying attention. Listening to these miniature moms, dads, sisters, and babies is a real lesson in life—yours that is!

Playing "school" can also be very simple to begin with. Making yourself the teacher you can give a lesson on colors, numbers, or whatever you want to, and it will be more fun than if you were plain ol' Mom at the kitchen table. Once Amy started school I would suggest *she* be the teacher; and during these games I found out that if you're bad you have to sit on a chair or stand by the wall, that art comes after snack time, and that turning off the lights means clean-up time. When she was old enough to play with friends, the game became more a social- than skill-oriented experience with paper monitors, teachers on recess duty, and lots of wrong answers resulting in notes home to the parents! Don't take it all too literally, though, because much of this school play is made up as they go along.

A pretend birthday party is a classic because by age three or four your child will have been invited to several and given one or two herself. Stuffed animals make excellent party guests; they are quiet and not likely to spill, and if you try not to think about how foolish you look in that silly pointed hat you just might enjoy youself!

You'll find that by imitating school, home, and party activities your child will understand better and feel some control over her future experiences. So join us now as we get Back to Basics!

✖️17✖️
Let's Play House

Equipment: Telephone and dolls (both optional).

Position: Each player should be in the area that she has made into a "house." Couch cushions make excellent walls, or you can fall back on the classic "playhouse"—a blanket draped over a card table.

Procedure:
1. Call your neighbor on the phone, "Ring, ring. Ring, ring."
2. Neighbor answers, "Hello?"
3. Begin a conversation. "What are you doing today? Is the baby sleeping?"
4. Neighbor answers the questions and, from her responses, keep the conversation going.
5. When no one can think of anything else to say, ask your neighbor if she'd like to come visit. "Why don't you come over. Have you ever seen my house? You can bring the baby!"
6. Neighbor accepts, goes out and locks her "door" and gets into her car (suggest that she act out putting the baby in the carseat, opening and closing doors).
7. Neighbor circles room, pretending to drive to her friend's.
8. When she arrives, greet your neighbor and show her around your "house." "Over here is the living room, and through there is the baby's room."
9. Offer her some pretend coffee or tea.
10. Begin a conversation about the difficulties of raising a family. "My baby cries all night! It drives me crazy. I give her a bottle, but as soon as it's gone, cries again!" Sigh heavily.
11. Neighbor picks up the tone of the conversation and adds her advice, "Well, sometimes you just have to let them cry a few minutes." Don't be surprised if the comments sound *very* familiar!
12. Announce that it's time for your baby's nap.
13. Neighbor says good-bye and "drives" home.

Suggestions: Since any kind of hideaway or special place is fun for young children, yours may enjoy making houses on her own.

Variations: Let's Play House was Amy's first experience at role-playing family members. When she was old enough to play with friends, this game took on a more traditional format. It began with "You be the mommy, I'll be the daddy," and continued with Daddy coming home from work, saying "Hi honey, I'm home!" while Mommy cooked dinner. Whether we like to or not, kids love to act out these stereotyped roles but we can encourage them to try variations such as Daddy taking care of the children or Mommy coming home from work while Daddy cooks dinner.

    A new dimension of Let's Play House could be the working mother who has to pick her children up at the sitter's!

❧ 18 ❧
School Days

Equipment: Chalkboard with chalk (magnetic letters are optional).

Procedure:

1. Suggest to your child that the two of you play "school." Ask, "Who do you want to be, the teacher or the student?"
2. The student needs a name. Let your child choose a name from her own class, use her own name, or pick a name at random. If it's a name from her class, a certain personality may accompany it!
3. Take your places. The student may sit in a chair or on a couch. The teacher stands at the front of the room.
4. Teacher says, "Hello class, today we are going to learn different colors."
5. Smart-aleck student jumps up and calls out, "I already know green and yellow!"
6. Teacher waves the student back into his seat saying, "Good Peter, but let's wait our turn!" (Preschoolers make icky-sweet teachers with sing-song voices, but when children in grade school play, the teacher gets crabbier!)
7. Teacher holds up two items and says, "Raise your hand if you know which block (or whatever) is red."
8. Call on a student to answer.
9. Student may answer correctly or wrong, on purpose.
10. Teacher continues the color lesson for a few more minutes.
11. Looking at the clock, the teacher realizes it's recess time! She instructs everyone, "Line up for recess!"
12. Student, depending on her game personality, can pretend to push and shove, or tell on someone who is!
13. Teacher reprimands the naughty child and sends her to end of the line.
14. Pretending recess is over, continue to snack time, story time, or art.
15. Ask for helpers to pass out juice or paints (all pretend). And don't forget monitors for the clean up.

Procedure:	**16.** Student responds to teacher's directions, asks questions ("When is snack time? Can I go to the bathroom?") and draws teacher's attention to those misbehaving ("Teacher! Johnny's not sitting down!") **17.** Now change roles. **18.** When either player tires of the game, pretend the school day is over.
Suggestions:	Whichever role you play, remember to ad-lib, keeping the game fun and light. Also, since your little teacher or student may get stuck during the game, watch for chances to whisper suggestions to her.
Variations:	You can add a second student in the form of a doll or teddy bear. The player acting as the students must speak for both! One of Amy's favorite versions of School Days consisted of her being "the naughty boy in class." Being a quiet student in real life, she loved this fantasy of running around the room, grabbing pencils, or talking out-of-turn! As teacher, she liked to continue the fantasy when I was the naughty boy. And the flip side of this is, of course, the good student. This student always is called on to "tell the others the right answer" and is used as an example to others, "Look how nicely Amy is waiting her turn." When you are teacher, use this opportunity to introduce letters or numbers. If your child shows an interest, play "school" more often!

❧ 19 ❧
Happy Birthday to You!

Equipment: A selection of toy plates, cups, and spoons (or use small paper plates). An assortment of party favors, hats, blowers, whistles, and the kinds of goodies given away at birthdays. (Juice, jello, or cheese are optional.)

Procedure:
1. Suggest to your child that today is the cat's birthday (or dog's, bird's, teddy bear's).
2. Help her set the birthday table. Set places for imaginary friends (neighbor cats?) or use dolls and stuffed animals.
3. If you have them, place a party favor and hat at each place.
4. "Ding, dong!" Answer the door and let in the party guests.
5. Seat the guests and help them put on their hats.
6. Time for the cake! Depending on the age of the guests, the number and the spontaneity of the game, the cake can be imaginary or something simple already on hand. Popcorn, nuts, jello, or raisins are good cake substitutes. Carry the "cake" ceremoniously out to the table.
7. Everyone sings "Happy birthday to you. . . "
8. Divide up the "cake" and enjoy! Whether you're using real or pretend food, smack your lips and rave about the delicious cake, not to mention the frosting!
9. Time for the games! Pin the Tail on the Donkey is a traditional party game and can be easily imagined.
10. Tie a pretend blindfold on a player, give a few turns, and head her off toward a pretend tail-less donkey!
11. Let your little player suggest and organize a game.
12. "Ding, dong!" Here are the moms to pick up their children.
13. Be sure your birthday cat says "Thank you" to her guests.
14. Part of having a party is cleaning up afterwards. Give your young child a job to help pick up.

Suggestions: Set aside a drawer or box where your child can save the various party favors she collects at birthdays. Save any left over invitations, party plates, or decorations from your own birthdays to use for pretend play.

If you have a record with "Happy Birthday" on it, play it!

Variations: One year Amy was given a white rat which she named Laurie. She made a wonderful pet and celebrated birthdays almost weekly. We became very accustomed to the call "You're all invited to Laurie's birthday!" and the sight of a beautifully set table with cheese on each plate. Encourage your child to set a theme for the party depending on the guest of honor.

Giving and receiving gifts played a very small part in these parties. If it was planned in advance (several hours) Amy would wrap some of her toys in comic book pages. If she didn't think of it until the last minute, she'd just bring out a toy, or draw a quick picture. And most of the time she forgot about gifts completely—the cake and the games being party enough!

The festive gathering doesn't have to be a birthday. Stage a wedding with lots of dancing!

After her daddy became an association board member, "meetings" with buffet-style refreshments became as popular as birthdays.

PART 5

✣✤✥✤✣

Places to Go, People to See

The games you'll find in this section are similar to those in When I Grow Up—realistic ones based on your child's awareness of her surroundings. They differ, though, from the occupational games in that entire scenes are recreated involving several different jobs. Restaurant is a good example and a likely place to start. You can trade off playing waitress, cashier, cook, bus boy, and customer; or play several parts, depending on how many people are playing. The equipment or props can vary. We've played Restaurant using big leaves for menus, rocks for food and small leaves for money, as well as with real menus, note pads, and plates. Actually, Amy enjoyed the rocks and leaves version best.

Games such as these can hurry along a slow dresser ("Let's pretend we're buying a party dress at the mall. Oh! How pretty. . .try this on!") or get the table cleared after dinner ("Hey! At this restaurant the waitress helps the bus boy!") How do you think I get Amy's shoes on or her skates laced up without a hassle? That's right! The old shoe store routine!

The games that follow are ones that appeal to our family, but there are many other possibilities. Next time you stop at the gas station or run into the bank, talk to your child about what you see and who does what. Not only will it give her something more to do than collect all the loan brochures, but she will have the background material for a game when she needs it!

Here are our favorite places to go and people to see.

❧ 20 ❧
Car Wash, Bike Wash; I Wash, You Wash

Equipment: Bike, sponge, bowl of sudsy water, hose, and a towel.

Position: Place bike(s) and other equipment on driveway, sidewalk, or patio.

Procedure:
1. Help your child design her "bike wash" along the same lines as a regular car wash. There should be several different stations during the wash process. The first station could be the soap suds and sponge, the second the hose, and the third the towel.
2. Set up these areas several yards from one another.
3. Line up the bikes at the car wash entrance.
4. Decide upon who's the car wash operator and who's the car owner.
5. Car owner pulls up to the first station and says, "I'd like a wash please."
6. Operator hands owner a ticket and tells her to pay the cashier.
7. Owner gets out of car (off the bike) and pretends to pay cashier.
8. Operator calls to owner, "Hey! You took the keys! I need them."
9. Owner returns keys to car and then stands around waiting for her car to be done, or she plays a double role and now works at the car wash with the operator.
10. Take the car through the different washing, rinsing, and drying stations.
11. When the car is finished the operator signals to the owner (who has switched back to this role) by a wave of the towel—you know how they do!
12. Owner thanks the operator and drives off!
13. Trade places and start over on the same or different role.

Suggestions: Create a dialogue between operator and owner: "Be sure to clean those handle bars," "You missed a spot on the tire!" or "Dry the seat carefully!" Operator responds "Yes, yes we always do an excellent job."

Variations: If you have several players, add more cleaning stations. A scrub brush and squirt bottle for tires is a good one!

Your car wash could double as a gas station, as most of them do. Fill it up before going through the wash!

❦21❦

Restaurant Fun

Equipment: Pencil, small pad of paper, paper or toy plates. (All equipment is optional, however.)

Procedure:
1. Call to your restless child, "Oh waitress! I've been waiting a long time for you to take my order!"
2. When your child gives you a puzzled look, continue, "Here's your order pad and pencil. This magazine will be my menu."
3. When your child is ready, give your order, "I'll have a hamburger, fries and milkshake. Oh! No onions please!"
4. Child scribbles on the pad, pretending to jot down the order.
5. Have your waitress decide on an area for the restaurant kitchen. She calls to an imaginary cook (unless you have more players), "Here's an order!"
6. Waitress waits a few moments, then returns to the customer with the order. "Here's your hamburger, lady."
7. Ad-lib a conversation, "Excuse me, Miss. You forgot my shake," or "Pardon me, but these fries are burned!"
8. After your order has been straightened out and you've eaten, ask for the bill. (You may have to whisper an explanation to your waitress. She's new on the job, you know!)
9. Pay your waitress with either make-believe cash or a credit card!
10. Talk to yourself as you leave the tip, "She did a good job. I think I'll leave a dollar tip." Be sure to thank her as you leave.
11. Now trade roles. As waitress you can add several new lines to the routine, for your little waitress/waiter to use next time. Try, "Are you ready to order?" "Is everything all right here?" and "Do you need a booster chair?"

Suggestions: While visiting with friends or relatives your child can "take orders" with a pretend order pad as well as bring out pretend meals, and all you have to do is pretend you're eating dinner out with friends.

Variations: If you have several players, they can trade off playing waitress, hostess, cashier, and customer. The hostess not only can seat the customer, and give out the menu, she can also put the customer's name on a waiting list.

Restaurant Fun can become quite elaborate if played in a sandbox or at the beach. In this version, making the food (literally *sandwiches*) is a major part of the game. Whether your child is playing alone or with friends, you'll probably be asked to sample carefully created pies and puddings. Smack your lips, Yumm, yumm!

When playing outside, use what's available for money, menus and plates (rocks, sticks, or leaves).

If your child is more interested in cooking than she is in serving, convert the restaurant into a bakery!

❧ 22 ❧

Market Day

Equipment: Toy shopping cart, small lunch bags, a doll or teddy bear, pretend food, and a toy cash register or pocket calculator.

Position: Market cashier sets up her check out station at a table or couch. Shopper stands by the cart.

Procedure:
1. Decide on who's the shopper and who's the cashier.
2. Shopper puts baby (doll or teddy bear) in the cart with instructions to sit quietly!
3. Shopper pushes cart around room pretending to fill the cart with groceries on her list.
4. Every so often shopper stops to remind baby to sit down or gives her a cracker.
5. Shopper comes over to checker and asks, "Where will I find the peanut butter, please?"
6. Checker responds "Oh, that's on Aisle 2B."
7. When shopper has finished shopping she comes to check out stand.
8. Checker takes each item out of the cart, names it and calls out a price. "Cheese, dollar fifty; milk, seventy five . . . ."
9. As she calls out prices she bangs away on her register.
10. Checker comes up with a final total and shopper pays—either make-believe cash or a check (if she uses a check the checker can call for approval!)
11. Shopper can help checker bag groceries.
12. Trade roles.

Suggestions: The shopper may forget something and have to run back to Aisle 3A at the last minute.

Variations: Add a player and you've got a box boy. When eighteen month old Katie wanted to play we called her our "box baby!" Remember, it's her job to help the customer out with the groceries.

❧ 23 ❧

The Shoe Store Experience

Equipment: Shoes

Position: Salesperson, who is holding shoes, kneels in front of the customer. A selection of shoes, yours and hers, is on display.

Procedure:

1. Some unhurried morning while your child is dressing say, "Pretend this is a shoe store and you try on shoes."
2. The salesperson (you) says, "What kind of shoe are you interested in?"
3. Salesperson asks customer to stand on an imaginary foot measurer and announces that the customer wears a size 10-1/2 (or whatever).
4. Pretending to look in the "back room" (bathroom?) salesperson returns with the shoes and says, "I think these will fit. Is the color okay?"
5. Customer responds one way or another and tries a shoe on.
6. Salesperson says, "Why don't you walk around a few minutes and see how it feels."
7. Customer decides it is fine, and salesperson puts the other shoe on.
8. Thanking salesperson, customer pays and leaves the store.
9. Now let the customer be the salesperson.
10. As customer you can add more dialogue. "Oh, these are too tight in the toe!" or "Don't you have these sandals in brown?"

Suggestions: If you are short on time, just pretend Shoe Store for as long as it takes to put on your child's shoes.

If your shoes aren't on yet, she can pretend to be fitting you with new shoes and then you're on your way!

If you have a shoe horn, use it!

If you've plenty of time, play the never-satisfied customer and try on several pairs before buying any!

When playing with brothers, sisters or friends, the salesperson can ask them all to "take a number" and grumble about how crowded it is. Call the store manager for help!

PART 6

✖✖✖✖

Who's Who

As I mentioned in the introduction, the games here are all based on the experiences of our family. Between the ages of three and four, Amy's favorite pastime was experimenting with different roles within the family. Sometimes she'd be baby, sometimes daddy and, often, mommy. Knowing what it felt like to be someone else helped her discover who she really was and where she fit in the family. Perhaps role-playing other personalities helped clarify her position as well as gave her a chance to give the orders instead of take them! When she was Mommy I was usually assigned the role of "a little girl who does something bad." I was not necessarily Amy, just some anonymous, naughty child. After sticking out my tongue or grabbing a pretend toy from a pretend friend, I would be reprimanded—and, oh, it all sounded *so* familiar!

It's inevitable when a new baby arrives that your older child will want to play "baby." All the books agree that this is healthy and normal, but how it can get on your nerves! Dealing with the daily routine of a new baby is exhausting enough without a preschooler crawling around on hands and knees, sucking on pacifiers and saying, "Goo, goo, ga. Me, baby!" Fortunately they grow out of this "baby phase" before too long, although at the time it seems like forever, and then you have that big brother or sister helper that you'd planned on all along.

I remember when Amy, age four, liked to pretend she was six or seven. "Pretend I'm six and this is a big girl bike," she'd say, patting her Big Wheel. What a refreshing change from that absurd baby imitation she used to do! Finally content with growing up, Amy was looking at what lay ahead for her instead of what had been. And I was proud of her because I know it really isn't easy to grow up and leave those carefree days of babyhood behind.

And then there was another twist to Amy's role-playing. It was sometimes a way of sorting out problems or confused feelings. The summer she was three I enrolled her in swimming lessons. Amy stuck it out for a few days, but then made the announcement that mothers everywhere dread hearing—"I don't want to go anymore."

Whether it be to school, to the babysitter's, or to piano lessons, it makes your heart sink because you must then decide whether to force your child to continue (teaching them responsibility, follow through, and all those good things) or let her off the hook (which is what you'd really like to do but are afraid will be damaging to her character and she'll be a "quitter" all her life!). In this case I decided to lay the foundation for responsibility and dragged my reluctant swimmer to her class. I admired the one parent who was able to pluck her whimpering child from the pool, deciding to try again next year. Oh, well, we continued on, and then every afternoon Amy would lug her big doll out to the living room and play "swimming lessons." Seating the doll on the coffee table, Amy would play the part of swimming instructor. "Jump in and use your big arms!" she'd say to the doll. Then, speaking for the doll, she'd cry "I don't want to! Mommy!" Switching from instructor to doll she would reenact her lesson. Interestingly enough, she'd calmly force the doll to swim the length of the living room, using her "big arms." There was also a variation in which Amy was the mom dropping the doll off for her lesson. In this version I was to be the child and Amy would tell me to "scream and fuss" as she pretended to walk from the pool to the railing where the parents were supposed to sit. Amy would smile sweetly, wave and call "You're okay! Do your big arms!" (where have I heard that before?) while I made the doll squirm and fuss at the edge of the pool.

I listened carefully to how she handled her roles, hoping for a clue as to what to do in real life! But most importantly, I learned that, for Amy, role-playing was necessary, and it helped her to play out these controversial scenes.

Here you'll find the games Amy played when she wanted to put the shoe on the other foot!

⚔24⚔
I'm You, You're Me

Equipment: None

Procedure:
1. Make the suggestion, "How would you like to be Mommy and I'll be you?" (Can't imagine a child who'd turn *that* deal down!)
2. Begin by asking your "Mommy" a question your child is always asking you. Imitate the tone of voice, too. "Mommy? Do I *have* to take a nap today?"
3. Your child will probably answer in a very cool, grown-up voice, "Yes honey. You know you do, *every day*. No arguing!"
4. Again, recalling past discussions along these lines, argue, "But Mommy, I've been good and I'm not tired!"
5. The game will depend on how she handles the situation. Amy used to tell me, "Pretend you are bad and won't take a nap. Say something sassy and I'll send you to your room!"
6. Follow your child's lead, and since you're pretending to be her, behave the way she does in this situation.
7. Your child may not want to act like you usually do or want you to behave like she does. Play it however she wants and pay attention—she may be trying to tell you something!
8. To wind the game down, give your child fair warning, "Okay, pretend I finally go to sleep and then the game will be over."

Suggestions: It's hard to say where it will lead. Amy usually directed the game, working out situations that were important to her at the time.

Variations: Picking a trouble spot between you and your child, with her as the mom and you as the child, can be very therapeutic, not to mention interesting. Since any number of situations fit into this game's structure, try eating dinner, going to bed, or getting ready for school.

You can "babysit" a doll while the mother (your child) goes to the movies. As babysitter, you have a dual role. You do the crying for the baby as well as portray the sitter who comforts her with "Don't worry honey, Mommy will be home soon." Your child will interpret the mother's role in her own style—staying home after all, because of the baby's crying; or going off happily, assuring the sitter, "She'll be fine as soon as I leave!"

On the lighter side, role-play an afternoon in the park or a day at the beach. In these positive situations you can pretend to show "your mom" treasures you've found or call her for help in doing a daring jump from the climbing gym! As "mom" your child may be able to feel the same sense of pride that you often feel—and perhaps you'll be able to empathize with your child next time she loses a newly found shell.

❧ 25 ❧
And What's the Daddy's Name?

Equipment: None

Procedure:

1. Let's say you've recently visited a friend's house, preferably one with children, and if your child doesn't think of it, suggest, "Remember when we were at Ann's? I could pretend to be her and who would you be?"

2. Picking up the spirit of the game your child names someone in the other family. "Okay, I'll be Elizabeth."

3. She would then match up other family members, "Katie is Jennifer, my doll can be baby Rebecca. . . ." But Amy always got stuck here and had to ask, "And what's the daddy's name?"

4. Once everyone is someone else, your conversation should include their names as much as possible. "Elizabeth! Go ask Jennifer if she wants a banana," or "Elizabeth! Tell Jennifer it's time to go to Amy's house!"

5. Your conversation, filled with questions, is determined by the activities, interests, and people of the family you are role-playing. Some questions that enable her to show off her pretend identity are: "How was second grade today, Elizabeth?" "I wonder when our daddy will be home from the doctor's office today," or, "Put that toy away in the room you share with Jennifer."

6. After you've exhausted all the pertinent questions that come to mind, suggest that your child continue being "Elizabeth" if she wants, but that she play outside or watch "Sesame Street."

7. As you regroup to go to the market, or take her to school, she may want to revive And What's the Daddy's Name. And, suddenly, you may be driving along in a VW bus with three kids and a dog, instead of a station wagon with two kids and a doll!

8. Give advance warning before ending the game. "When we get to the market, we're through playing this" or "I have to make a phone call in ten minutes and then we're done." And stick to it or you'll go crazy playing "Ann" all day!

Suggestions: A toddler, included in the game whether she likes it or not, may become confused with her new identity. If you call her by a pretend name, follow up with "That's *you* Katie! This is a game! You be Jennifer, okay?" If she becomes upset, and this will depend on her age and mood, work it out so she can be her *real* self.

A plus for this game is that you can play along while otherwise occupied. Since you're role-playing a family setting, keep on sewing, mowing the lawn, or paying the bills while you talk!

Variations: Bored with family friends, Amy liked to "be" someone from school. Although it was a school friend, we played that we were home and that I was the mom. Not knowing a whole lot about the family, our conversation was pretty general—so remember to use the pretend name often. One year Amy had two boys, Justin and Dustin, in her class. Although they weren't brothers, she was convinced they were, and wanted Katie to be Dustin while she was Justin. But I could never keep them straight, and the game began to get on my nerves just as Justin (or was it Dustin?) moved away!

Your child may want to role-play a neighbor friend or someone from church.

✿ 26 ✿

Me, Baby!

Equipment: None

Procedure:

1. Whether you encourage it or not, somewhere along the line your child will want to pretend to be a baby again. Having a new baby in the house will influence the extent and frequency of Me, Baby! You'll recognize step one when your child enters the room at a crawl or stagger and announces, "Mommy! Me, baby!"
2. Your best bet is to go along with it. "Oh! My goodness! Look at this cute baby!"
3. Your "baby" will most likely gurgle, coo, or cry in response.
4. Pick her up and hold her over your shoulder as if she were an infant. Pat or rub her back while you sing a quick verse of Rock-A-Bye Baby.
5. Pretending the couch is a crib or bassinet, lie her down with an imaginary bottle. "Here's your bottle, baby. You just lie there and watch Mommy wash the dishes!"
6. When your "baby" tires of lying still she may fuss or cry.
7. Take the imaginary bottle away and hand her a toy or keys to play with. "Play with this, baby. Mommy can't hold you right now."
8. Next time she "cries" pick her up again or rock her in a rocking chair.
9. A good way to end is simply to put the "baby" to bed. While you pretend to put on her pajamas, talk to yourself, "Boy, I sure will be glad when you are a big girl. I wish I had a big girl who could talk and play and help me. I'm awfully tired of babies!"
10. If your child wants to continue the game, tell her that babies sleep most of the time!

Suggestions: If you have a new baby at home, having your older child play Me, Baby may be nerve-wracking! But if she really wants to act like a baby, let her, emphasizing how boring it is to be a baby who can't eat cookies or ride bikes!

An older sibling who wants frequently to play Me, Baby is probably working out some jealous feelings, so include the daily songs, baby talk, and loving that you give the new baby in the game with your older child.

Variations: When little sister Katie became a crawler, getting into things she shouldn't, Amy liked to play Me, Baby as an older baby who I was supposed to say "No, no!" to all the time. She also developed a taste for the teething biscuits Katie never liked! So when you're tired of one baby stage, suggest that she go on to toddlerhood the next time you play. Pretty soon you'll have her back to normal again!

❧ 27 ❧
You're a Big Girl (Boy) Now!

Equipment: None

Procedure:
1. As a welcome change from Me, Baby or just for fun, say, "Hey! That's an awfully big bike (or hard book, puzzle, or game). You must be six-years old!" Pick an age at least a couple of years older than she really is.
2. As your child gives you a puzzled look, whisper "Let's pretend I don't know you and you really are a big six-year-old."
3. As your child shifts into a more grown-up stance and puts on a serious face, say, "Are you really six? Can you really ride that *big* bike? (put together that hard puzzle. . . .)"
4. As she confirms all this, ask her to show you.
5. Act impressed with her tremendous riding, reading or puzzle-solving ability! "Wow! You really are a big girl!"
6. To carry it further ask, "Are you in second grade?" (or whatever)
7. She responds with a smug "Yes."
8. Further impressed, you say, "Isn't it awfully hard?"
9. Of course she declares it's a breeze for her!
10. Ask her where she lives and comment, "Wow! Are you big enough to cross the street by yourself?"
11. She can, of course.
12. Continue along this line, asking her about things you know she longs to do!
13. When you can't think of anything more to ask her, tell your "big girl (boy)" that it was nice talking to her but you have to get dinner for your family now!

Variations: We stumbled across a variation in which your child must convince you she's six (or whatever) because you don't believe her! The dialogue goes something like this: Your child says, "Hi. I'm six."

And you answer, "Oh, no way. You couldn't be six. If you were six you'd know how to . . . (think of something she can do) count to twenty and *I know* you can't do that!"

After she does indeed count to twenty, you are very impressed ("Wow! I didn't think you could!") but still not convinced ("But I still don't think you're six because if you were, you'd be able to do a forward roll and *no way* can you do one!") until you're finally convinced that she must be six!

PART 7

❧✖✖✖❧

Story Hour

One of the wonderful things about telling a story is that you can do two things at the same time. It isn't necessary to stop what you are doing to tell a story to a child who is upset, sick, or just plain bored. On a busy day when there has not been any special time for the kids, you can always fall back on the "Quickly get in the car so I can tell you a story" routine. Stories can also be told while fixing dinner, changing diapers and folding laundry.

You can tell a story about most anything, but children's favorites will always be those about themselves, real or make-believe, past, present or future; and those stories about you, when you were little. Telling a story of this sort can stir old memories as well as plant new ones in your child's mind. Amy and I both enjoyed a sense of continuity derived from stories about her as a child and then those about myself as a child.

Retelling a favorite book or poem will be more involved if your little listener wants to act it out as you go along. We used to do the *Wizard of Oz* as we walked the dog. The sidewalk was, of course, the Yellow Brick Road and we met the Scarecrow, Tin Woodman and Cowardly Lion in the form of two trees and a bush. When telling stories or acting out books, the question of whether or not the characters are real will inevitably be asked. When reading fairy tales, scary witches or mean giants were immediately identified as imaginary in order to allay young fears. But dismissing Superman, Peter Pan, and (worst of all) Mary Poppins as make-believe could be a mistake. Pretty soon someone's going to mention Santa Claus and then you're in big trouble! Parents have to decide where to draw the line with fantasy figures—not an easy task to do.

We came up with our own formula for answering these questions. Since I, personally, would like to believe in just the slightest possibility of magic, we explained that scary things that worried our children were pretend, but that unique, special magic (that worked for good) perhaps did happen a long time ago and, you never knew, might happen again someday!

What you'll find here are the stories I came up with when asked, "Mom? Tell me a story."

𝔷𝟚𝟠𝔷

Once Upon a Time

(The Penelope/Paul Stories)

Equipment: None.

Procedure:
1. If your mind draws a blank when asked to tell a story, try this, "Once upon a time there was a little girl named Penelope (or boy named Paul)."
2. Penelope is really your daughter (or Paul your son) and the story should follow the events of her day. "Penelope woke up early and had raisin bran cereal for breakfast. Then she had to clean her room."
3. At this point your child will figure out your story game. "Hey! That's me! This is about me, isn't it?"
4. Of course you deny it. "You? What makes you say that? This isn't you!"
5. Continue your story, explaining how Penelope then played with her friend next door (use the friend's real name) or whatever your child actually did that morning.
6. More cries of "I knew it was me!"
7. Suddenly change the story with some make-believe: "Then Penelope and her friend discovered a secret tunnel that led to a king's palace!"
8. If your listener likes it, continue the drama. If not, stick to reality.
9. Wind up the make-believe portion of your story, with Penelope back home again: "And after Penelope tamed the dragon she said good-bye to the king and she and her friend ran back home through the tunnel in time for lunch."
10. The story ends with Penelope doing exactly what your child is doing at the moment. "And after the market, her mom told her a story!"
11. "That's me again!" your child will notice.
12. Admit it, "Yes, I know. It's really all about you. I saw you sneak off into that tunnel. I heard that dragon roar!"
13. Now you've got her really mixed up! Quit the teasing, give her a hug and go on to something else.

Suggestions: This game is a good distraction for someone with a skinned knee, bad dream (leave out the dragon and add a birthday party) or hurt feelings!

Variations: You can tell a story of pure fantasy but use the names of her real family and friends.

✻29✻

When I Was Your Age

Equipment: None

Procedure:
1. To convince your child that you, too, were young once, tell her a story! Think of a situation similar to hers to begin. "When I was four, my mom (your grandma) used to let me help make cookies" (or whatever you happen to be doing).
2. As you continue, make the story coincide with her feelings. "I used to always want tastes of the batter and she'd say 'If you stick your finger in there again you can't lick the batter.' And I could never understand why it bothered her." This being, of course, exactly what I say to Amy every time we make cookies!
3. Your child will perhaps ask you, "Did you help stir like I do?"
4. Describe what it was like to help your mom make cookies, keeping the experience very similar to your child's.
5. Include people in the story she knows, "My brothers, your Uncle Bob and Uncle Jeff, always wanted to lick the bowl. And my dad, your grandpa, always ate the most cookies."
6. The story will continue, depending on your child's reactions and questions.

Suggestions: It's more fun for both of you if you use real stories. You'll be surprised what you can remember about those days way back when!

There's either the spur-of-the-moment story told to cheer up the discouraged child learning to ride a two-wheel bike, or the requested story at bedtime. In either case, what your child will probably want to hear is that you were sometimes naughty, sometimes sad, and sometimes happy.

Amy's favorite When I Was Your Age stories were about my not wanting to go to bed, my mother crushing an aspirin in sugar when I was sick, and hating to have my Band Aids pulled off so much that I would hide in my closet.

Variations: You may get off the subject and end up discussing "Where was I when you were four?" or "Where will you be when I'm a mommy?" Good luck!

Children also like to hear about when you were a tiny baby or ten-year-old, or even a teen-ager! This may remind your child that she was a baby once and she'll want a story about those good ol' days.

Amy liked hearing about falls and close calls, as well as trips we took and games we played. And after telling a story about yourself as a ten-year-old, tell her a story about what *might happen* when she's ten! Amy enjoyed hearing how she would walk to school with her little sister and go on airplane trips to visit Grandma!

❧ 30 ❧
What Would Happen If. . .

Equipment: None

Procedure:
1. When your child is dawdling and you hear yourself say, "Hurry up! You can't go to school in your nightgown" she might respond "Why?"
2. And this is how we discovered the What Would Happen If. . . . stories. "Well, if you went to school in your nightgown your teacher would say 'Amy, didn't you forget something? Your clothes!' and the other kids would be very surprised to see you still in your nightgown!" And so on.
3. Remember, the whole time you are distracting your child with this story, you should be subtly dressing her for school.
4. Don't make it sound too much like fun, or she'll want to try it! "You probably won't be allowed to paint or play at recess because your nightgown will get in the way."
5. Use your imagination to exaggerate the story, "And since you have the nightgown on, your teacher will think it's night time and send everyone home to bed!"
6. When your child is dressed, finish up your story. "But since you're all dressed you won't have to worry about everyone thinking you're silly!"

Suggestions: This story game is a good way to answer that constant "Why?" question, especially when they already know the answer and are just using the question as an excuse to dawdle.

Variations: You can tell a What Would Happen If. . . story about never washing your hair (spiders might live in it) or eating your dinner (too weak to chew gum) or getting gas in the car (run out of gas on the way to Disneyland).

Reverse the roles and ask your child to tell *you* what would happen if. . . .

❧ 31 ❧
Storybook Land

Equipment: None

Procedure: 1. When Amy had a favorite story or book, she liked to make it come alive! For starters, choose a simple story like "The Three Little Kittens" or "The Gingerbread Man."
2. As narrator, begin the story, "The three little kittens had lost their mittens and they began to cry. . . ."
3. Your child will be the kittens, saying, "Oh Mother dear, we sadly fear. . . ."
4. And then it's back to you, "What! Lost your mittens, you naughty kittens. . . ."
5. You're not only reciting the lines, but acting them out as well, shaking your finger while you scold your "kittens."
6. Your child then pretends to hunt and find the mittens. "Oh Mother, dear, see here, see here, our mittens we have found!"
7. Complete the story and then trade characters if you want.

Suggestions: If you have a pair of mittens handy, the game will be more fun. The use of props is up to you. You can set up a bowl for pretend washing, a clothesline for pretend drying or even something sweet for the "Then you shall have some pie" part!

If her favorite story is extremely long, like "The Wizard of Oz" or "Pinocchio" then limit Storybook Land to just one or two scenes.

We enjoyed doing "The Three Little Pigs" because one person can be all three pigs as the wolf blows her from house to house! Sometimes our houses were just imaginary areas and sometimes we found sticks and rocks for houses.

Doctor Doolittle books and many of the Berenstain Bears series work nicely, too.

Variations: Then, through television, Amy was introduced to "The Super Heros" (Superman, Wonder Woman, Spiderman, etc.). We would either act out a story she'd seen on television or make up our own dramatic Wonder Woman-to-the-rescue story!

PART 8

Spontaneous Fun

You never know what will strike their fancy. The car can be a roller coaster, the hose a snake, or the mail truck a charging rhinoceros. When you least expect it, children will invent an incredibly imaginative game. That's what Spontaneous Fun is all about.

Other than go along with them, adding new dimensions to the games, there isn't a whole lot for you to do. If you have a highly realistic child, however, you may want to lead the way in Spontaneous Fun, teaching her how to find the extraordinary within the ordinary. A child stuck in a rut, always pretending the same thing, can also be encouraged to find new adventures.

The best spontaneous games are made up by several children playing together. As they bounce ideas off one another, each new thought sparks another. Their conversations are filled with "I know what!" and, "I have an idea!" as they work their way through battles, shipwrecks and space flights.

And they learn all kinds of fascinating things from each other as each child contributes ideas from his or her own experiences. Coming home from a preschool field trip, one boy was shooting off imaginary torpedos at passing cars. Sure enough, the next time we were in the car Amy took over the torpedo controls. After a mile or so she asked, "Mom? What *are* torpedos?" But, until they are playing with their own friends, you'll be the one "bouncing ideas" and looking for a spontaneous game with your child.

There are only a few games in this section because, basically, the game should come from the child herself. But if you need some ideas on how to get started or want to know what to look for so you'll recognize it when it happens, use the following games, straight from Amy's imagination, as a guide.

✖ 32 ✖

Bears In a Cave, No Way Out

Equipment: None

Procedure:
1. While eating breakfast in the kitchen, Amy would suddenly say, "Hey! Let's pretend we're bears."
2. Sometimes I'd try to get out of it by saying, "Oh alright. I'm hibernating."
3. "No! It's spring and this could be our cave!"
4. "And the door is opening, right?"
5. She'd pause while deciding who she wanted to play it. "No. There's no way out!" and her eyes would sparkle.
6. "Oh dear, but what will we do for food?" I'd play along.
7. "We *have* food right here" and she'd indicate the refrigerator!
8. So I'd think of another problem, "What about water? We'll *die* without water!"
9. Once again she'd find the solution—the sink, of course!
10. And I'd continue to think up the problems we'd face as bears in a cave with no way out. There was, "What if the phone rings?" (but Amy pointed out that we have an extension in the kitchen) or "How will we visit Grandma?" (to which she shrugged her shoulders and said, "Can't!").
11. Finally she'd show the "secret passage" that led to the outside world. Whew! I was beginning to suffer from claustrophobia!

Suggestions: Most of the time Amy rejects the ideas I want to add to the game, probably because she wants it to be all her own, but often what I've said will give her a new idea. So don't think she doesn't need your suggestions just because she doesn't use them!

Variations: The game may take many twists during its course. We once played that other bears would try to enter the secret passageway and we had to determine which were good bears (they could come in) and which were bad (they must be kept out!). Sometimes they wore imaginary signs around their imaginary necks and Amy would announce "This one says NICE," and sometimes we had to rely on whether or not they had good manners. A bear who grumbled "Hey! Let me in!" was most likely bad!

Remember, though, your child will come up with variations that suit her own personality.

❧ 33 ❧
Pillow Panic

Equipment: Couch pillows or bolster pillows from a day bed.

Position: Lay the pillows in an open area on the floor. Player stretches out on top of pillows.

Procedure:

1. Pretending that the pillows were a boat, Amy would gently sway back and forth on the pillows, imitating the rolling motion of a boat at sea.
2. Suddenly she plunged overboard!
3. "Help! Help! There are mean crocodiles that are trying to bite me!" she would call.
4. She would scramble back up "on deck" having had a very narrow escape.
5. Again the "boat" would rock back and forth.
6. And again Amy would be thrown overboard! Only this time, she'd roll off the opposite side of the pillows.
7. "Oh, no! Hurry before the crocodiles get you!" I'd warn her.
8. But she had a different idea. "Let's pretend that on *this* side there are nice crocodiles and they swim over and give you candy!"
9. And she'd proceed to thank the crocodiles for the candy as they helped her back on board.
10. At this point I'd join the game. "Well! I'd like to get into this game! Do those nice crocodiles have any chocolate bars?"
11. Whether joining her on her pillow, or setting up my own boat, we'd both teeter back and forth before tipping over into either the cruel waters filled with angry crocodiles, or the imaginary sea of sweet-toothed crocodiles.
12. The game usually ended by waving good-bye to the nice crocodiles, scolding the mean ones, and setting our sails for home.

Suggestions: A lot of dramatics, squeals of delight and fear, add to the excitment.

Talk to your child as you play, asking "I wonder why those other crocodiles are so mean?" or "I wonder where these crocodiles get all the candy." This may give her some new ideas for the game.

If you're not comfortable with candy-giving crocodiles (Amy, who thought of this, has a bit of a sweet tooth like her mom), change them into kiss-giving creatures.

Variations: Sometimes a mean crocodile would swim over to the nice side and trick us! And one time, the waters became infested with sharks who smelled the chocolate, and we had to head back early.

❧34❧
Don't Look Now, But . . .

Equipment: None

Position: In a car

Procedure:
1. As Amy rode in the back of the station wagon with her little friend, Evan, they'd watch for cars following us.
2. Suddenly Amy would say, "Don't look now, mom, but there's bad guys behind us!"
3. "Yeah! In that green truck!" Evan would add.
4. "Uh oh! Did they rob a bank or escape from prison?"
5. Sometimes they liked my ideas and sometimes they had ideas of their own. Evan watched a lot of TV and often came up with things like, "No, they are spies and they stole the secret spaceship plans!"
6. "Yeah!" Amy would go along with it and add, "And the police are in that blue car!"
7. "Well, I'm getting out of here," I'd say as I turned into the park.

Suggestions: As you or the cars in your game turn corners or stop at red lights, you'll have to readjust the game and find new participants!

Variations: The game doesn't have to be a chase scene. You can suggest that your car is leading a parade in which each car following you is a different marching band or float.

CONCLUSION

And now that you've sampled the different games and helped your young child learn to pretend, you're about "pretended out," right? Well, the great thing about fantasy play is that children actually have more fun playing with other children than they do with their not-nearly-as-enthusiastic parents. And the older they get, the more they enjoy sharing in the fun with their friends. So don't panic if you feel you can't face another "physical" by your resident doctor or one more tea party crammed into those tiny chairs; she'll soon discover that her friends are more willing participants, with more unique variations than you could ever come up with.

Awkward three-year-olds, however, at a stalemate in play will gladly accept an adult suggestion to play "house" or "hospital." And with very little supervision they'll be able to play together, while you catch up on the newspaper, if your child feels comfortable and confident pretending.

But when she gets older, don't lose your touch completely! I always found it fascinating to play "house" or "school" with an older, more worldly Amy who'd been playing with her friends, who'd become the leader, teaching me the tricks of the trade.

But if for no other reason than just to have fun, pretend play is important to you and your child. The memories brought back, the independent play skills developed, the intellectual and creative stimulation offered are nowhere near as important as the precious time well spent with your rapidly growing children.